Workbook

Editorial Offices: Glenview, Illinois • Parsippany, New Jersey • New York, New York
Sales Offices: Parsippany, New Jersey • Duluth, Georgia • Glenview, Illinois
Coppell, Texas • Ontario, California • Mesa, Arizona

www.sfsocialstudies.com

Program Authors

Dr. Candy Dawson Boyd
Professor, School of Education
Director of Reading Programs
St. Mary's College
Moraga, California

Dr. Geneva Gay
Professor of Education
University of Washington
Seattle, Washington

Rita Geiger
Director of Social Studies and
    Foreign Languages
Norman Public Schools
Norman, Oklahoma

Dr. James B. Kracht
Associate Dean for
    Undergraduate Programs
    and Teacher Education
College of Education
Texas A&M University
College Station, Texas

Dr. Valerie Ooka Pang
Professor of Teacher Education
San Diego State University
San Diego, California

Dr. C. Frederick Risinger
Director, Professional
    Development and Social
    Studies Education
Indiana University
Bloomington, Indiana

Sara Miranda Sanchez
Elementary and Early
    Childhood Curriculum
    Coordinator
Albuquerque Public Schools
Albuquerque, New Mexico

Contributing Authors

Dr. Carol Berkin
Professor of History
Baruch College and the
    Graduate Center
The City University of New York
New York, New York

Lee A. Chase
Staff Development Specialist
Chesterfield County
    Public Schools
Chesterfield County, Virginia

Dr. Jim Cummins
Professor of Curriculum
Ontario Institute for Studies
    in Education
University of Toronto
Toronto, Canada

Dr. Allen D. Glenn
Professor and Dean Emeritus
College of Education
Curriculum and Instruction
University of Washington
Seattle, Washington

Dr. Carole L. Hahn
Professor, Educational Studies
Emory University
Atlanta, Georgia

Dr. M. Gail Hickey
Professor of Education
Indiana University-Purdue
    University
Ft. Wayne, Indiana

Dr. Bonnie Meszaros
Associate Director
Center for Economic Education
    and Entrepreneurship
University of Delaware
Newark, Delaware

ISBN 0-328-08173-6

18 19 20 21-V004-14 13 12 11

© Scott Foresman **K**

Contents

Unit 4: Our Big Book of Earth

Unit 5: Our Big Book of the U.S.A.

Unit 6: Our Big Book of Family Stories

Use Illustrations

 Circle.

 Draw.

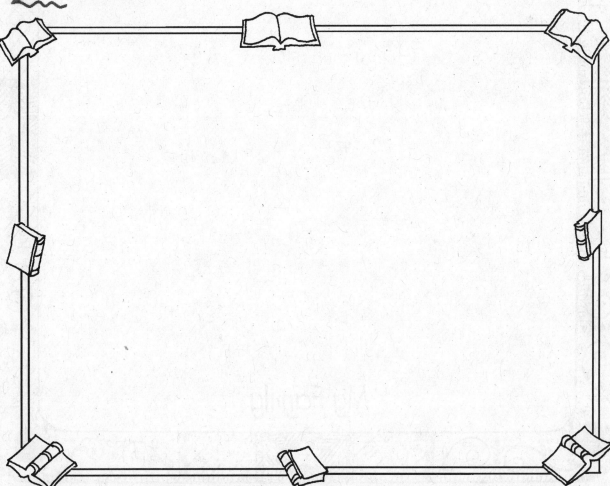

 Directions: (Top) Circle the picture that tells more about this sentence: *I like to play soccer.* (Bottom) Draw a picture to go with this sentence: *We read books at school.*

 Home Activity: Ask your child to tell what is happening in the uncircled pictures above. Help your child create sentences that tell about the pictures.

© Scott Foresman **K**

Families

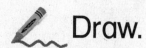 Draw.

My Family

 Directions: Draw a picture of your family. Share the picture and name the people in your family.

 Home Activity: Look through family photos and help your child identify family members; for example: *This is my mother, your grandmother. This is my brother, your uncle.*

Name _____

Homes

 Draw.

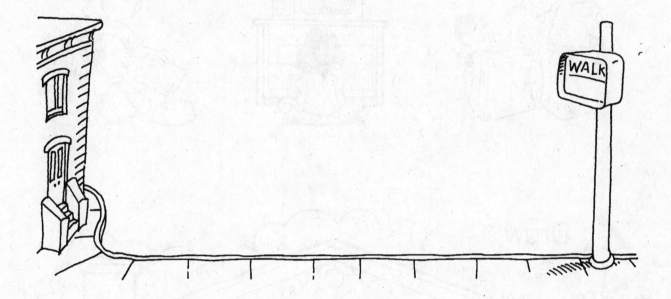

 Directions: (Top) Draw a picture of a kind of home you might see in a city. (Bottom) Draw a picture of a kind of home you might see in the country.

 Home Activity: Look through books or magazines for pictures of homes. Decide with your child if the home would be found in the city, near a city, or in the country.

© Scott Foresman K

Getting Along

 Circle.

✏️ Draw.

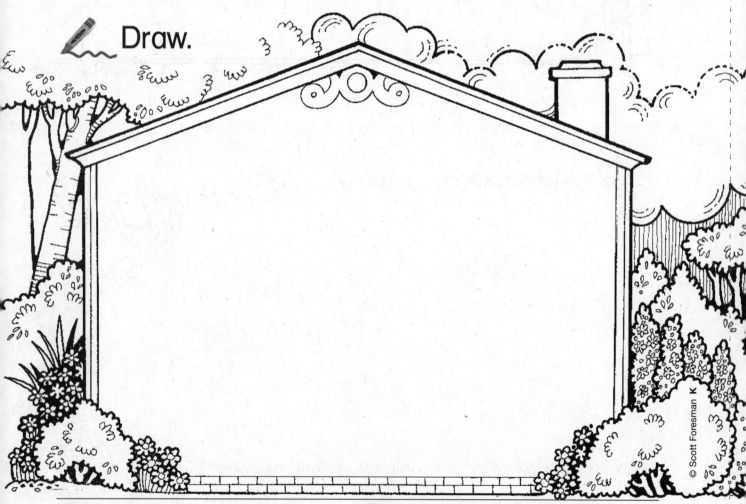

 Directions: (Top) Circle the pictures that show how children can help at home. (Bottom) Draw a picture to show one thing you do to help at home.

 Home Activity: Talk about jobs and/or responsibilities your child has and that you have. Decide on ways you and your child might be able to help each other.

Solving Problems

 Look.

Draw.

 Directions: Look at the pictures. What problem do the children have? (Both want to swing.) Draw a picture to show one way the children might solve their problem.

 Home Activity: Think of a household problem you and your child can solve together. Name the problem and discuss different solutions. Choose the best one and put it to use.

Name _____

School Helpers

 Color.

 Directions: Look at the pictures. Color the
pictures that show school workers.

 Home Activity: Ask your child to tell you about
his or her favorite school helper. Then share a
story with your child about your favorite
teacher or school helper.

How are people alike and different?

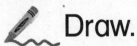 Draw.

Alike

Different

 Directions: Draw a picture to show one way in which you and a friend are alike. Then draw a picture to show one way in which you and a friend are different.

 Home Activity: Talk about how members of the family are alike and different.

© Scott Foresman K

Classify/Categorize

 Color.

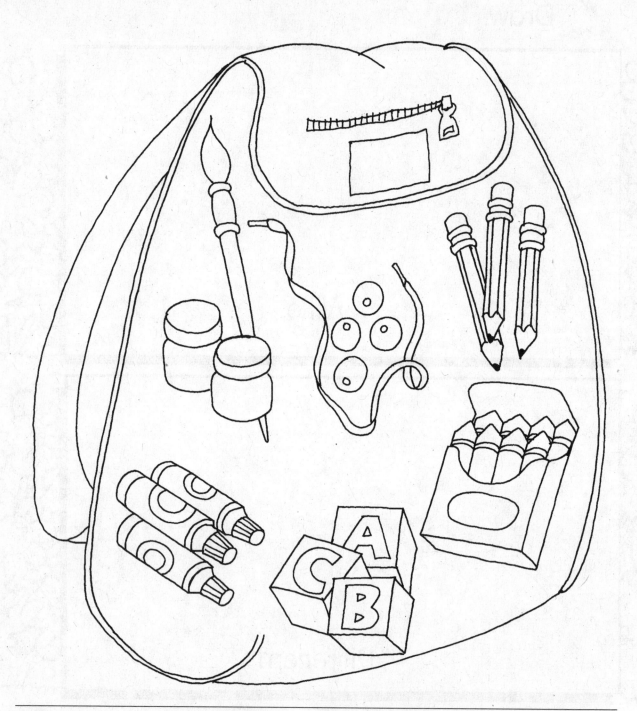

 Directions: Look at and name the pictures: *paintbrush and paints, beads, pencils, markers, blocks, crayons.* Color the things that you can use to make pictures.

 Home Activity: Help your child classify and categorize with sorting activities such as putting away silverware, matching socks, grouping toys, putting away clothing.

© Scott Foresman K

Workbook

Neighborhoods

 Draw.

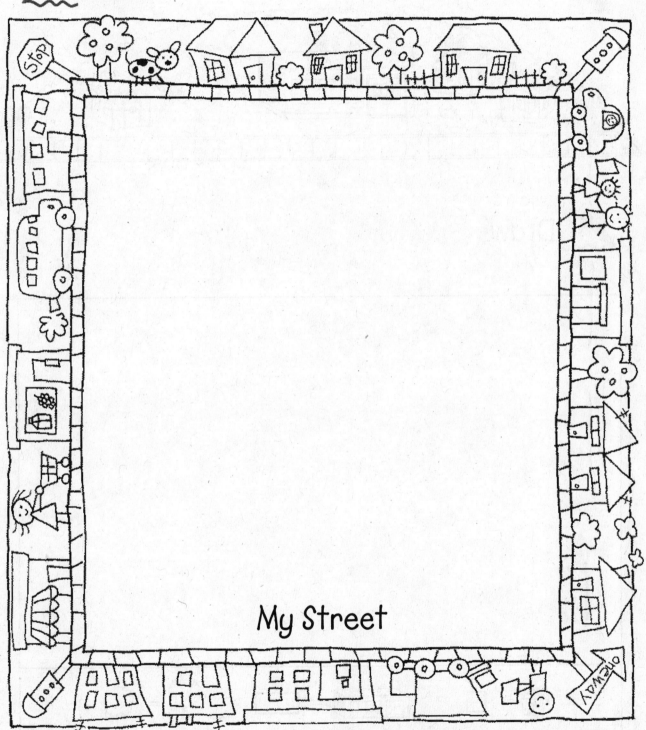

My Street

 Directions: Draw a picture of your neighborhood. Share the picture with the class.

 Home Activity: Take a walk around the neighborhood with your child. Help your child identify buildings and signs along the way.

Maps

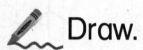 Look.

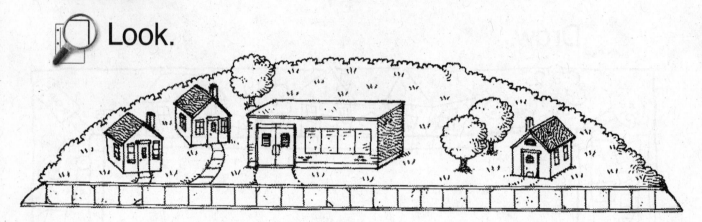

 Draw.

 Directions: Look at the picture of the neighborhood. Draw a map to show the neighborhood. Use the shapes to help you.

Home Activity: Help your child draw a picture map of your neighborhood or street.

© Scott Foresman **K**

Name _____

Signs

 Cut.

Directions: Look at the pictures.
Think about what sign is missing from each
picture. Cut out the sign and paste it with
the correct picture.

Home Activity: Help your child look for signs
around your neighborhood. Look for picture
signs as well as print signs.

Rules

 Look.

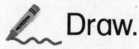 Draw.

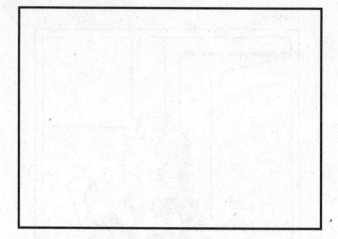

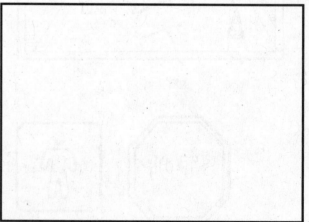

 Directions: Look at each picture. Decide what rule the animal is not following. Draw a picture to show what is wrong.

 Home Activity: Help your child review rules that should be practiced in and around your neighborhood.

Name _____

Community Helpers

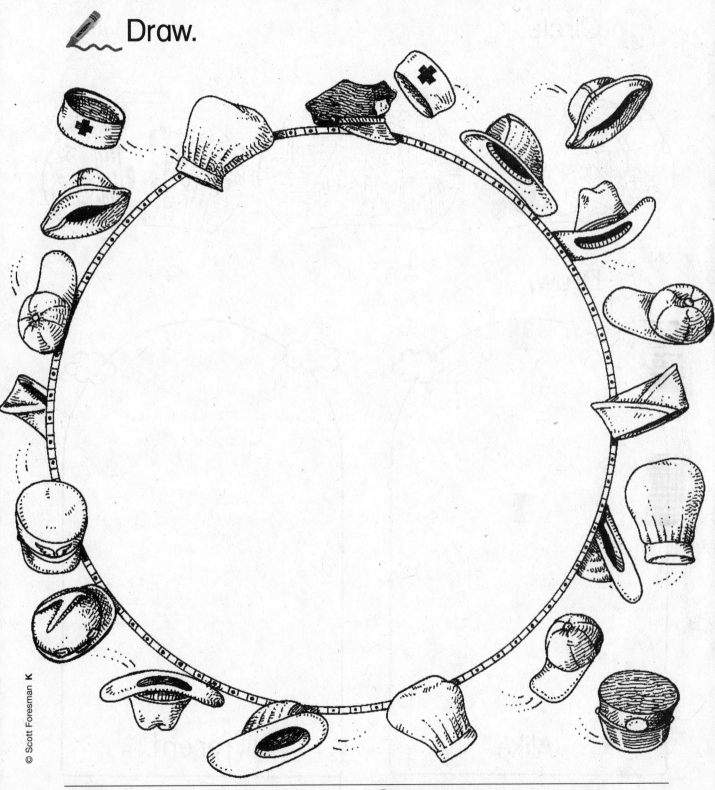

✏️ Draw.

 Directions: Draw a picture of a person who helps in your community. Share your picture with the class and tell what you know about that community helper.

 Home Activity: Help your child become familiar with the uniforms of community helpers in your neighborhood.

Name _____

Communities

 Circle.

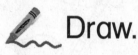 Draw.

Alike

Different

 Directions: (Top) Circle the picture that looks most like your community. (Bottom) Draw a picture to show how your community is like that community and how it is different.

 Home Activity: Tell your child about communities you have lived in. Describe how they were similar to and different from the community in which you now live.

© Scott Foresman K

Celebrations

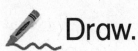 Draw.

 Directions: Draw a picture of a celebration you like. Share your picture with the class.

 Home Activity: Talk about family celebrations with your child. Note traditions and customs your family observes. Invite your child to add a new tradition to a family celebration.

Name _____

What is a community?

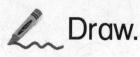 Draw.

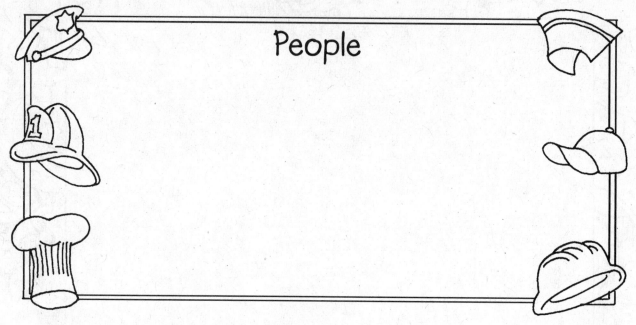

People

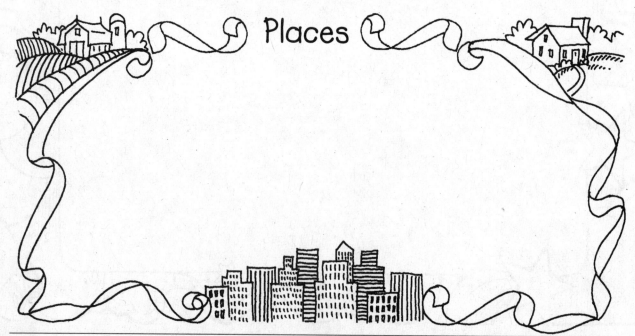

Places

 Directions: (Top) Draw a picture to show a community worker. (Bottom) Draw a picture to show where your community is—in the city, in the country, or in the suburbs.

 Home Activity: Invite your child to share what he or she has learned about your community. Share your knowledge of the community with your child.

© Scott Foresman K

18 Big Book 2 Unit Review

Workbook

Name _____

Compare and Contrast

 Color.

 Directions: These twins are having fun at the school fair. Look closely at the twins to see what is alike and different. Color only the things that are different.

Home Activity: Help your child compare and contrast items or places in your home. Find ways in which clothing, furniture, books, or rooms are alike and different.

Work

Draw.

My Job

 Directions: Draw a picture of a job you have at home. Share your picture with the class.

 Home Activity: Talk about jobs family members have at home and outside the home. Discuss how these jobs help the whole family.

Name _____

Jobs

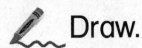 Draw.  Write.

Someday I want to be a _____.

 Directions: Help me name the jobs these children would like to have. Draw a picture to show what job you would like to have. Write a word to complete the sentence.

 Home Activity: Invite your child to talk about what job he or she would like when older and why. You might share information about jobs that adult family members have.

Jobs Then and Now

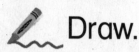 Draw.

 Directions: Look at the picture. It shows what a classroom looked like then, or long ago. Draw a picture to show what a classroom looks like today.

 Home Activity: Talk about how schools have changed since you were a child. You might mention that there were no computers or that records were used instead of cassettes.

Earning Money

 Draw a line.   Write.

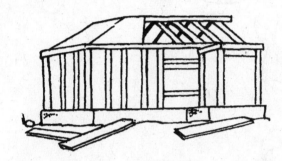

People earn money at _____.

Directions: Look at the pictures. Draw a line to match the worker to the job he or she does. Then write a word to complete the sentence.

Home Activity: Look through magazines to find pictures of different kinds of workers. Talk about what these people do to earn money.

© Scott Foresman K

Using Money

 Draw.

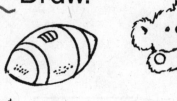

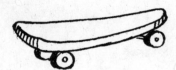

 Circle.

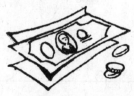

 Directions: Draw a picture of something you would like to buy. Circle the money if you can buy it now. Circle the piggy bank if you need to save your money to buy it.

 Home Activity: Help your child save for a simple item that he or she would like to buy. Your child can decorate a jar in which to save the coins he or she earns.

© Scott Foresman K

Making Choices

 Color.

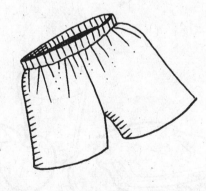

 Directions: Look at the pictures in each row. Color the picture of what you would choose to buy. Share your reasons with the class.

 Home Activity: The next time you go shopping with your child, talk about the choices you make when spending money.

Needs and Wants

✏️ Color.

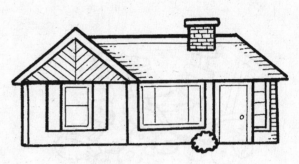

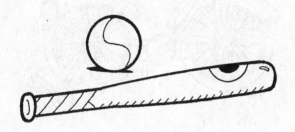

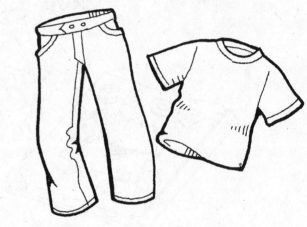

© Scott Foresman **K**

 Directions: Think about the things that people need and the things that people want. Color the pictures of things that people need.

 Home Activity: Your child is learning about the basic needs of food, clothing, and shelter. When shopping with your child, help him or her distinguish wants from needs.

Needs/Food

 Draw. 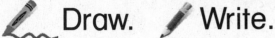 Write.

My favorite food is _____.

 Directions: Draw a picture of your favorite food. Write a word to complete the sentence. Share your picture with the class.

 Home Activity: Ask your child to explain why food is an important need. Invite your child to help you plan and cook a family meal.

Needs/Clothing

 Color.  Write.

SALE!

People need _____ .

 Directions: Color the part of the picture that shows something people need. Write the need to complete the sentence.

 Home Activity: Ask your child to explain why clothing is an important need. Talk about clothing items that are needs versus clothing items that are wants.

Name _____

Needs/Shelter

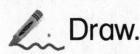 Draw.

 Directions: People need food and clothing. They also need shelter. Draw a picture to show a shelter that people need.

 **Home Activity:** Talk with your child about the importance of your home. Ask your child why it is important for your family to care for your home.

From Here to There

✂ Cut.

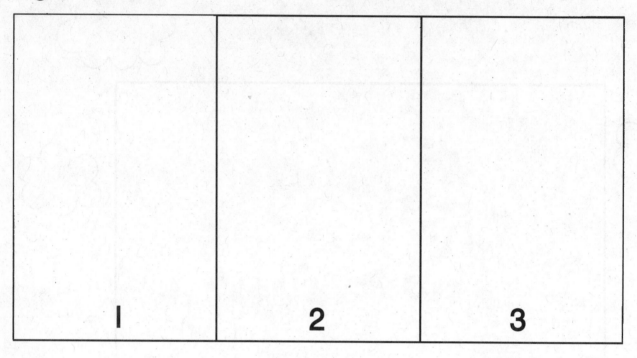

1	2	3

 Directions: Talk about the pictures at the bottom of the page with me. Cut out the pictures. Paste them in the correct order to show the work people do to bring you milk.

 Home Activity: Help your child find out about the work that goes into making and transporting his or her favorite food.

What kinds of work do people do?

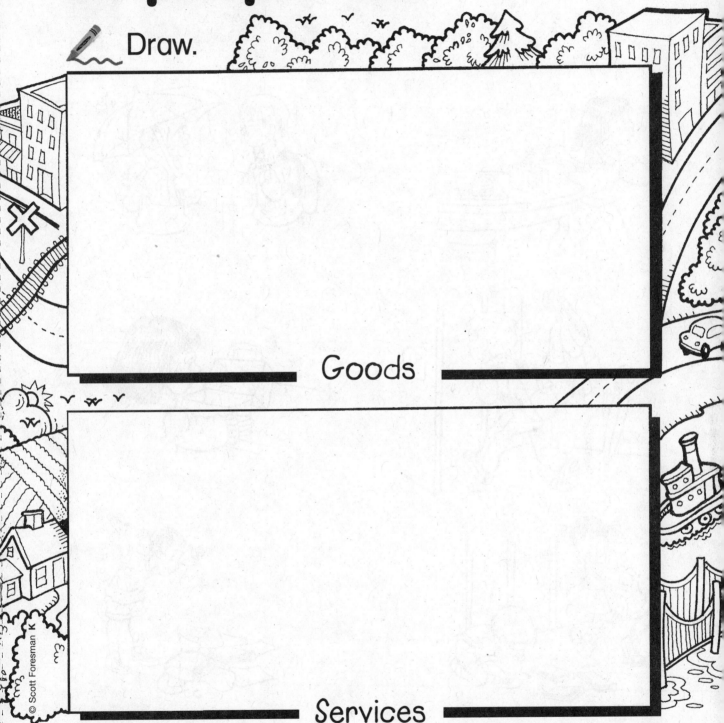

Draw.

Goods

Services

 Directions: (Top) Draw a picture to show a job that produces goods or makes something. (Bottom) Draw a picture to show a job that helps people in a community.

 Home Activity: Invite your child to share what he or she has learned about the kinds of work people do.

© Scott Foresman K

Name _____

Cause and Effect

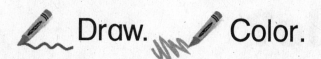 Draw. Color.

© Scott Foresman **K**

 Directions: Look at each picture. Draw a line from the first picture in each row to the picture that shows what happened. Color each picture that shows what happened.

 Home Activity: Help your child identify cause and effect by asking *why* to his or her actions, for example: *Why did you get a glass of water? Why did you answer the phone?*

Weather

 Draw. Write.

I like _____   days.

Directions: Draw a picture of your favorite kind of weather. Write a word to complete the sentence.

Home Activity: Talk about activities your family enjoys during different kinds of weather: sunny days, rainy days, snowy days, windy days.

Seasons

 Draw.

Spring

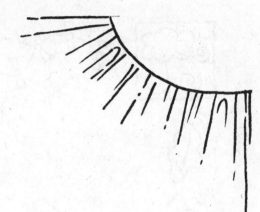

 Summer

Fall

Winter

Directions: Draw a picture to show what you like about each season. Share your pictures with the class.

Home Activity: Discuss with your child the season in which different family birthdays fall.

Name _____

Forests

 Draw.   Write.

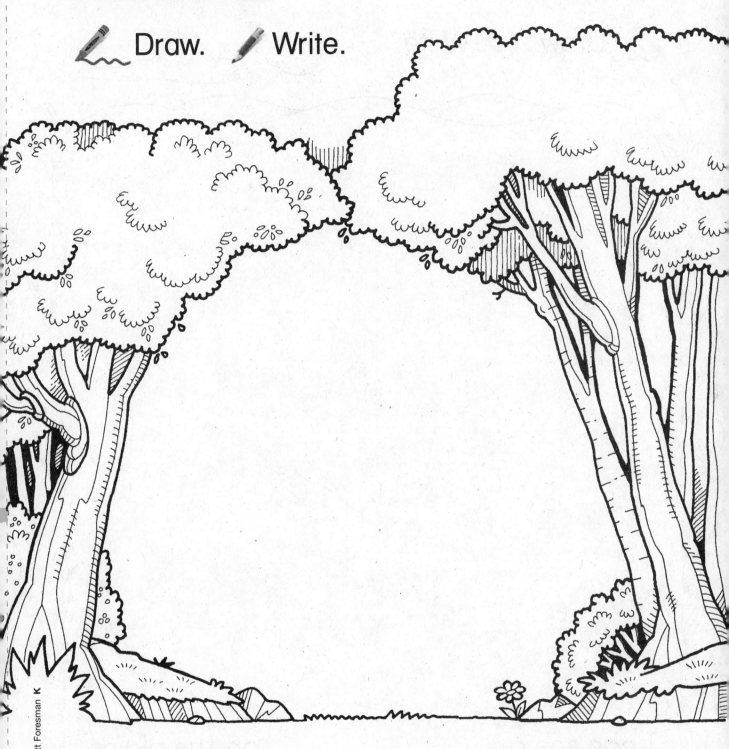

© Scott Foresman K

I can see a _____ in the forest.

 Directions: Draw a picture of an animal you might see in the forest. Write an animal name to complete the sentence.

Home Activity: Invite your child to share what he or she learned about forests. Talk about experiences you and/or your child have had in the forests.

Plains

 Draw. 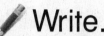 Write.

I can see a _____ on the plains.

 Directions: Draw a picture of an animal you might see on the plains. Write an animal name to complete the sentence.

 Home Activity: Invite your child to share what he or she learned about the plains. Talk about experiences you and/or your child have had visiting the plains.

© Scott Foresman K

Mountains

 Draw.  Write.

I can see a _____ in the mountains .

Directions: Draw a picture of an animal you might see in the mountains. Write an animal name to complete the sentence.

 Home Activity: Invite your child to share what he or she learned about mountains. Talk about experiences you and/or your child have had in the mountains.

Name _____

Oceans

✏️ Draw.   ✏️ Write.

I can see a _____ in the ocean.

 Directions: Draw a picture of an animal you might see in the ocean. Write an animal name to complete the sentence.

 Home Activity: Invite your child to share what he or she learned about oceans. Talk about experiences you and/or your child have had in or near the ocean.

Workbook

World Map

 Color.

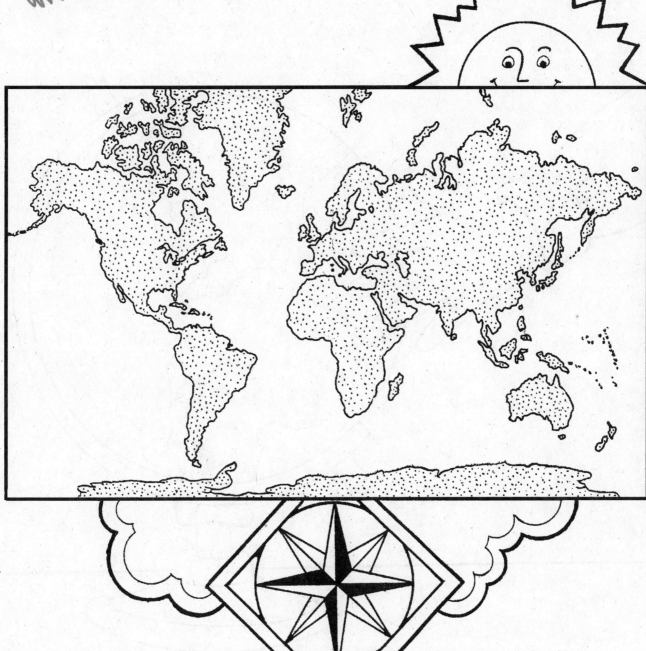

 Directions: Color the land areas of the world map green. Color the water areas blue.

 Home Activity: Have your child point out the land and water areas of the world map. Help your child locate the United States on the map.

Name _____

Globe

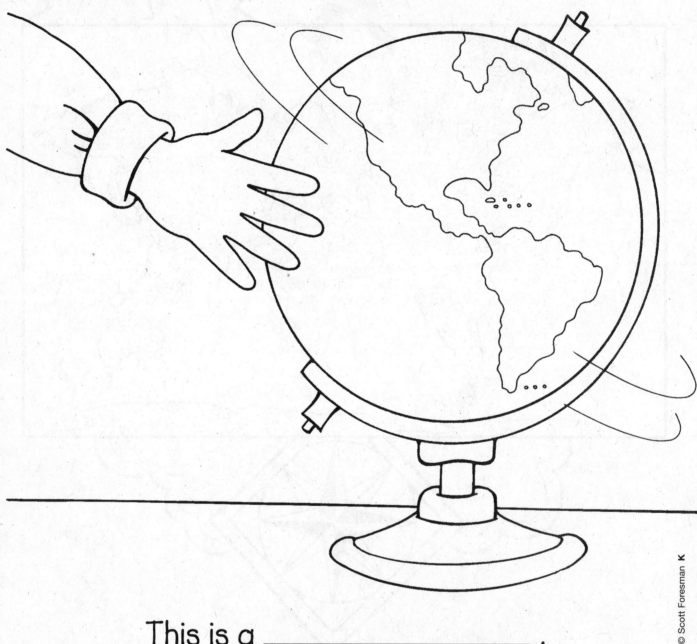 Color.   Write.

© Scott Foresman K

This is a _____ .

 Directions: Color the land areas on the globe green. Color the water areas on the globe blue. Write a word to complete the sentence.

 Home Activity: Help your child create a globe by using a marker to draw land areas on a grapefruit. Have your child tell why only half the globe can be seen at one time.

Workbook

Conserve Resources

 Color.

 Directions: Color the pictures that show children helping the Earth.

 Home Activity: Ask your child to tell how each person on the page is or is not helping the Earth. Talk about ways you and your child can help the Earth.

Name _____

What does our Earth look like?

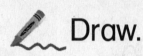 Draw.

On the Earth.

On a map.

© Scott Foresman K

 Directions: (Top) Finish the picture. Draw more things to show a place on Earth. (Bottom) Finish the map so that it tells about the picture of Earth you drew.

 Home Activity: Invite your child to share what he or she has learned about the Earth.

First Americans

 Color.

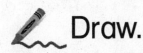 Draw.

 Directions: (Top) Color the pictures that show things used by Native Americans long ago. (Bottom) Draw a picture of something that Native Americans made with clay.

 Home Activity: Talk about each Native American article with your child. Invite your child to identify the resource used to make each item.

© Scott Foresman **K**

Explorers

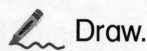 Draw.

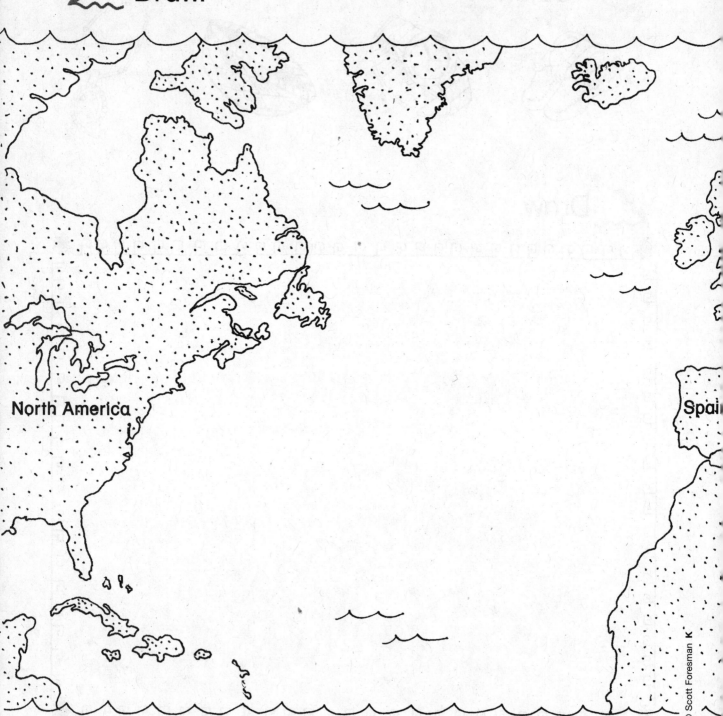

North America

Spai

 Directions: (Part 1) Draw a picture to show how explorers came to the Americas. (Part 2) Draw an arrow to show which way they came.

 Home Activity: Invite your child to share with you what he or she has learned about early explorers.

Name _____

Thanksgiving

 Draw.

A Thanksgiving Meal

Directions: Draw a picture to show a Thanksgiving meal. Share your picture with the class.

Home Activity: Ask your child to tell you about the Thanksgiving feast the Pilgrims and Native Americans shared. Help your child compare that meal to your family's Thanksgiving meal.

Celebrations

Draw.

I like to _____.

 Directions: Draw a picture to show one way you celebrate the Fourth of July, our country's birthday. Write about your picture.

 Home Activity: Ask your child to explain why Americans celebrate the Fourth of July.

Name _____

Changes in Travel

 Color.  Cut.

Then   Now

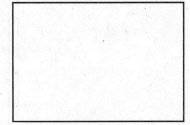

 Directions: Color the ways to travel. Cut out the ways people travel now. Paste them next to the ways people traveled then, or long ago.

 Home Activity: Talk about the ways your child has traveled. Share how travel has changed since you were a child.

Scientists and Inventors

 Circle.

| Now | Then | Now | Then |

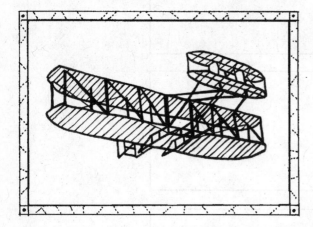

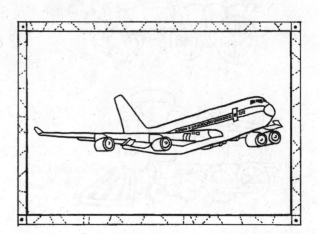

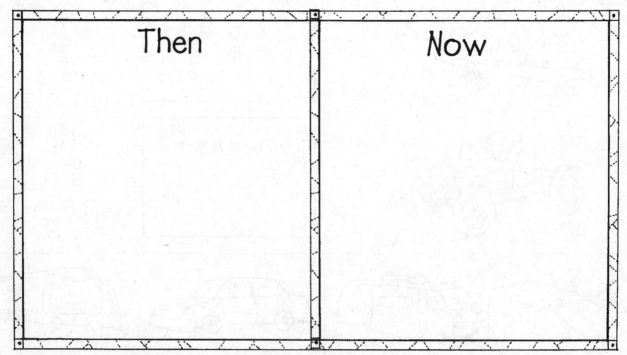

Then   Now

 Directions: (Top) Circle Now or Then to tell about each picture. (Bottom) Draw pictures to show how something you use every day has changed.

 Home Activity: Help your child see that all things change. Talk with your child about changes that have happened in your family or home.

© Scott Foresman **K**

How has our country changed?

 Draw.

Then

Now

© Scott Foresman K

 Directions: Draw a picture to show something about our country long ago, or Then. Draw a picture to show something about our country Now.

 Home Activity: Invite your child to talk about his or her drawings. Ask your child to tell you about other ways in which the United States has changed.

Recall and Retell

 Draw.

 Directions: Think about your favorite story. Draw a picture to recall the story. Use your picture to retell the story to a friend.

Home Activity: Help your child recall a family story or activity. Invite your child to retell the story in his or her own words.

Family Celebrations

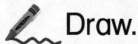 Draw.

 Directions: Draw a picture to show a family celebration. Tell a story to go with your picture.

 Home Activity: Invite your child to recall and retell the story that goes with his or her celebration picture. Recall other family celebrations with your child.

© Scott Foresman **K**

Then and Now

 Color. Cut.

Then   **Now**

 Directions: Color the pictures. Cut out the pictures of things families use today. Paste them next to the things families used Then, or long ago.

Home Activity: With your child, take a walk around your home. Share how different items in your home have changed since you were a child.

Special Foods

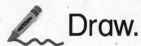 Draw.

   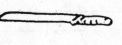 

 My family's special food is...

_____ .

   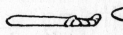

Directions: Draw a picture to show a special food your family enjoys. Finish the sentence to tell about your picture.

Home Activity: Invite your child to tell what makes this food special. Share your thoughts about foods or recipes that have been passed along in your family.

Games

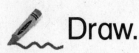 Draw.

© Scott Foresman K

I have fun with my _____.

 Directions: Draw a picture to show one way you have fun with your family or someone in your family. Then write a word or name to finish the sentence.

 Home Activity: Your child has learned that families can have fun when they work and play together. Talk about work and play activities that your family enjoys.

Places We Go

 Circle.

 Draw.

We have fun at the _____.

 Directions: (Top) Circle a picture to show a place you would like to go with your family. (Bottom) Draw a picture to show your family having fun at that place.

 Home Activity: Plan a family outing with your child. You might choose one of the places shown above or choose a place that you and your child enjoy visiting.

What is special about families?

 Draw.

My family is special.

Directions: Draw a picture to show one way your family is special. Share your picture with the class.

 Home Activity: Invite your child to talk about his or her drawing. Share family stories to talk about how families work, play, and learn together.